Here,
Which Is Also a Place

Mark DuCharme

Unlikely Books
www.UnlikelyStories.org
New Orleans, Louisiana

Here, Which Is Also a Place

Unlikely Books
www.UnlikelyStories.org
New Orleans, Louisiana

It is not the monotony of nature but the poems beyond nature that call to each other above the poets' heads. The heads of poets being a part of nature.

—Jack Spicer

Ecology *is* relationality, hence endlessness…. [It is] a thought-process that tends toward waxing and ramification. So does Poetry. Poetry is that writing which most persistently shakes off the Expected at every mini-step. It's open to anything, at any point. Ideally, each syllable is like Blake's "world in a grain of sand" (sound).

—Jack Collom

Et j'irai loin, bien loin, comme un bohémien,
Par la Nature,— heureux comme avec une femme.

—Arthur Rimbaud

No news
Is good news
On planet earth

—Sun Ra

Here,
Which Is Also a Place

I

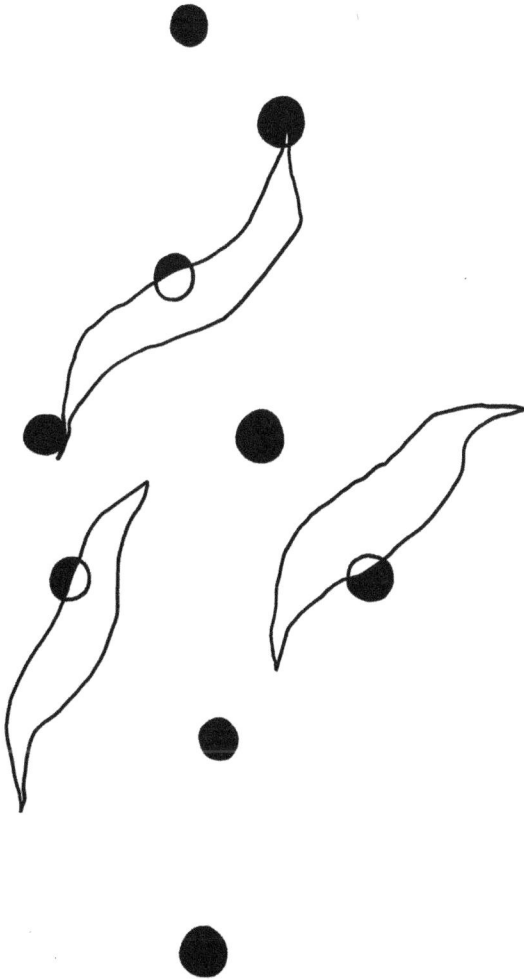

This earth is not yet won
This body, a tremor
       in earth-erupted jade

Searing violently
       until gone
When restless noon wakes

§

Light, which disappears into the traffic.
It is an agency in place of what's
Unformed— the tug of place

Ignites hidden spaces—
On the scale of going about

In the places of already

I don't know what this belongs with

§

The names of things frighten us
Into speech

Mouth of sky
Stuffed with newsprint

& The hiss where we
Abandon it

Toward edges of a window or name

～

The name is the animal name of skies

It is the air we keep repeating

Mouth of (an unnamable) debris

～

The read is full of noise
                (*Read* rhymes with *bled*)

It is inserted in the gape

To listen with fictitious praise

To bleat a horrid

        retort to silent

           repeating

To go on through the roofs of cities still not

                  knowing what to say—

        ~

The mind is arranged by very small things

Underscore the billions with the billions

Erase light with a song fracture

Breath of heat or day resumed

§

To be given wholly
To the creation of shadows,
False names & forgeries,
Images which vanish from the frame

To speak voicelessly
In confined spaces,
In sunken rooms
Where no one dwells

Night is an instrument for
Measuring the content of
Shadows, vowels' weight,
Reflections' densities

If you speak, look behind the door
To make sure no one is listening;
If you dream, become scalded
By objects' vivacity in sunlight;

If you speak, only do so
Little by little
Until the poem at the end of the frame
Causes you to be submerged.

§

To evaporate like speech, exchanging
       Physicalities for breath

Writing on the back of the   cat, it is
    An ultraphysical
Non-memorizable
     Event

We incorporate tense errors into our desires
        (*We incorporate tense* eros—

     Who swelter, then go briefly
  Into dark

Into densities which become matter—
      Although you are not here
Although we study the shapes of the   horizon, the hidden

    To think in tactile measure
Or become seared with reverb

     As noon's brightness burns
        In the scorch of the visible

§

The world is heavy with architecture. It is weary of place-
                                        [names, the need
                                                to inhabit.

Night is the construction   of the space between narratives

I have a secret to tell you:
Conjugal / Conjugating / interval (the Internal slant [meant]
                                                    [skidding

> *When we are gone, bring*
> *The necessary futures,*
> *Smoke stuck to fingers,*
> *Lovers with the time to breathe.*

§

Afield, the poem sweetened

In breath withheld, indulgent—

        to cause a swoon

At the very order of the marrow

At the parts of summer that a

        bee resolves—

Exemplar of form

§

In the stray conditions of what carries
Us forward to delight

The mind thinks in the form of
The poem, not the book

What goes toward you with so much heat
Will fill you with its gaping

The mind is a barrier
Tilted nowhere

Knowing— in this slim
Containment we call home

§

If I were a river I would flow
Through your city & nourish it. If I—

If I were a river
I'd be as polluted as love

& Fluently speak a second language.
If I could sing, I would be the sea,

But if I could flow, I would be unmapped
& Surround your environs 'til love breaks free.

§

It rains on us when we are near our feet
In disasters where we flower
When we move inside of flame
But disperse into redacted matter
Which is no longer blue, or near you

Then listen to the laughter of what's named
Where a gentle breeze impales us—

These ghost-scratchings on paper—
Blurry ink, the light remembered

§

We reflect the past in order to feed on it—
    Dislocating the splintered
      Inflections of winter
Which fuse with space & light

In an horizon without meaning   to extend
    The clangor of words swarming

Words only swarm when getting ready   to attack

To swallow the ocean in order to drown
    The name meaning nothing
      But its own weight

        In fields of flowers swelling—

§

Reservoir of noons crushed.
Singing is fleeing? but I am lost
To send you back to earth's forests
Until death becomes like night or gardens

§

To inhabit a space between futures
To erase the past unkindly
Decimating species, the earth's weight
Filled with scenes I've never been in

Does one die of memory? & Is it sudden?
Evoked in a fever or lane
Spelled like nightly volitions of violence
Where a city breathes, but no one dwells

———————————————

To inhabit a space between furtive violence
Sutured newsprint   evaporating impact
In the remains of the trees
Who are now departed

Does memory die
Evoking reckless grammar
In the still-departing forests
Whose very surface breathes,
        Becoming violently hidden?

§

This nostalgia for leaves' rustling
Evokes improper silence
Proper science

The event falls backward
In order to free up action
A nostalgia for leaves' rustling

Be afraid, if you insist
Insist on a more legible domain
At disarrays of deep night pending

The remains of all dislocating laughter
At fluttered edges of heat or day

§

The wind is suddenly among us
It does not fill our glances
Though we sleep
As fiercely as it often did.　The wind

Is a form of preying—
A kind of animal, an intense presence lurking
From the scale of timeless being
A remote mirror from which nothing's hung

To invent a weightless grammar
Where even devils lurch
In the unforgiving dust, toward which
Silence is the first hurdle

§

To be as transitive as translations of the moon's impact on

[waves

If you believe
Or are despoiled
As the souls of trees who are not listening

To live or leave, despoiled by fractured
Architecture—
& Everything else which falls apart
In the loss which leaving recreates

Where all is glass—
Is in us, still. Listen to it— here

Laugh where you want to, & then fall

Down

In distant ocean's salient

Weave

§

There is no book, only

A record of activity

~

Cars on freeways

At all hours

Surging

Like sharks who must go on

~

While history sends

A text

    & Whiny pop songs drone

~

& Rain on car windows reflects

Birds alight on power

Lines (there is no

Power)

        ~

A flash & a trickle—

        A flesh—

Dull pain blooming streets

        ~

The world's a stillborn   bloom

    Is all

         Is extant   ~~breath or mirror~~

      An *extent* of light

             Shattered—

Whirls in the whorl of streets—

Interstices inter-

        sections spirals—

Burnt afternoon forms

~

Does knowledge encompass us (you/me)
Making particle waves of hummingbirds' thoughts
In bright afternoon rain?

~

It's amazing where one can write poetry
It's amazing where one can't
In this jittery early-century
Which perforce must drown
All silence

        Solitude & connection—

~

While cities keep
    Accruing & gyrating

& Palm-waves waft

   In hazy, bright sky

& Impatient earth rustles

& Empurpled tree

    Boughs

Do a breezy shimmy

Above the traffic

    Dancing

   ~

       We are whom we

        Became—

       Inconstant as a

        Daisy

        Or piece

       Of tune skipped—

   ~

Even if we spill

    Our breath— & we will

Later than sooner—

This now is not over—

Of a waning afternoon, under elm shade—

    In this still-uncertain day—

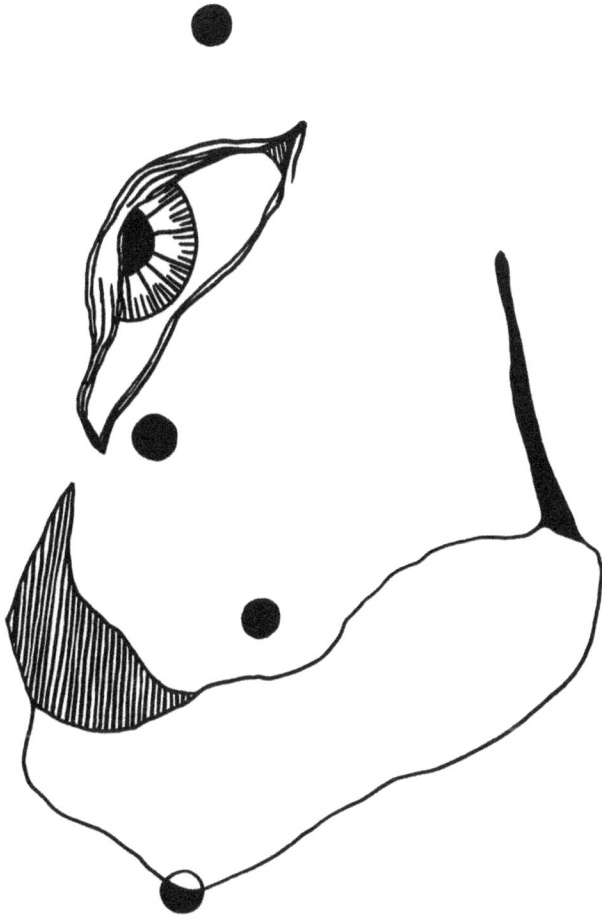

II

To make a map of the mind at
Unrest—
Who in the end has nowhere, no

Caravansary of flowers, no events, no fleeing
Where one left off
In desert light dissuaded.

The mind knows
Where it is going— usually.
Let it find you.

Better, prove
Worthy of the flush, the
Onrush (visually)—

Until all learning's curved
In reclamations yet
Unbidden.

§

I had already developed
This sense of what
To say at such instances, as they
Move from sorrow clutching

The pen in its
Conclusion stripped
Under the table or over the
Chair— to say as much,

A sense of this
Incomplete in the air

§

Or looking out the other
Way
In whatever form this silence takes—
This silence makes us full

At last, not needing other
Tropes or loan words
From the cohesion
Polyglot surfacing Braille

On the tongue, being one

In participatory voices

All as one, until you

Sang bleeding nearer

To the core of bone &

Spittle say you say all & I

Will sing & disappear

Into the rhythm skein unnerving

§

"And pass our long love's day. Landscape rushing away."
—*Ted Berrigan*

The landscape, in fact, does not rush away;
It is capaciousness, to fill
Gushing expanse until the moon's
At brim— & then it empties
Us of sameness crashing
Toward a mirror or lake.
It is the whole tune, a song imploding
Heard densities of clatter;
It is the coarse texture of the earth's genitals;
It is a way of knowing, or being held down
At the gape of hardness gnawing
Toward horizon's edge.

It is a swaying fixity to linger
At the bend
Of a syllable, but it also fills
Up with ocean's laughter—
Raw eyes toward night peering.

§

In the extraction of what lingers
Alongside night's lanky machines
To hinder the desire to go nearer
The place with its artificial frictions,
Its greedy, tedious lanes.   In the

Extraction of what follows
Underneath the waves
Until you were gnawing or blaring outside
The depopulated window where we stood
Performing acts of complicated grace

Leaving then, without a trace

§

And so going on
In the order one is given
To know these things wholly
In the depths of the body

A gaze or recurrence
Held up to mirror
To let the light enter
Corners of the given

Knowing it, putting it
Up to reflected knowing
The edges of your mouth
An intimacy with the gravest sparrows

If ever you are cracked, stillborn
Gaze thou into the space of nothing
Further between coherences (stymied)
While we lie selfishly between

§

To go on making faces at the screen
Speaking as of night, while we
Derive anterior postures, a means
Of drawing breath from tides

Night is longer than our eyes
& Comes in useless jolts
The words of people passing from our sight
The comfort of the despised

To enter night, become dispersed
In rain, or imitate those falling
Out of windows, off the wings
Of planes

Unravel passage to upheaval

Tread by vanishing light

§

Being here or
Elsewhere. Grief,
Which makes us full

With light.
Shitty, manmade things
Sinking in the original.

The tongue curves. One is
Being useful to one's
Self

In the act of hunger,
In the grief
Which ties us

To waking sight.

§

To think outside
Until it freezes
Elsewhere in the original

It is also important to heave
What phones
Cleft of place, but still portending

Garments of the very shrill
Ridiculous cupcake, my ghostly
Thief

Will you come in here
To wake the unlively
Bereft of windows which still don't shake?

§

Dark of sky
At afternoon—
      Earth
            Subject to vanishing

The shadow of   the shadow of elsewhere
Exacted by the pull
          Of now—

Lie there &   astonish me
With noon in your teeth while the wind moans

A worn-out tune—

       To wither;

    Then witness such

           Leaves scatter—

§

To get through to the back
Of the page
Until the air is bright

Is white
Like all dead forms
All flaming hindrance, all stopped material

Any fool knows that a flame
Cannot be held
Down

Yet what fools devour, a flame returns
One hundred thousand times over, never
The same

Drowning in its own retractions,

Its reflections, reimagined cities,

Faded restaurants & investigations,

A persistence never to return.

§

It is better to write something brief, imperfect.

It is better to write something which is

It is better to write

Torn apart, largely—

Creating in a

Chain.

§

Something there was, forgotten as shadow

As poetry is generally forgotten

Then tread lightly, in the sun

& Gather wildness when things aren't done

§

"I am a citizen of somewhere else."
—*Nathaniel Hawthorne*

I need something more than this silence.
Words gather about the place
Like hornets nesting in the rafters,
Like screamers thrown off balconies.

What we mean is so little—
Parsed, fragmented subjects
Not daring to sit still. To sit
Swallowing what little breeze

There is, if there is anything
Which the wind enjoins us to do,
Letting it out until we are through
In the earth-impacted elsewhere.

§

Yet being *here* is exactly the
Point
Toward which the efforts of the reader
Of the poem can't be won.

To be here, or mocking

In this sudden amusement,

This visible departure, its

Skirmishes & alibis

In cold earth gnawing

Toward a capture so inhabiting

I'd carve it from your whispers

Until the thin moon sank

Until the world was full of yellow surprises

& We walked the earth like captors

Of our own imaginations chaining

Flesh to syllable as easily

As the carved earth can't be won

§

Here, or clods of them
Draining the atmosphere
Of its mirth—
Draining our departure
Of its knowingness—
Draining earth
Of yellow surprise.

When you are surprised,
Enter the garden,
Put your weight on
A daffodil.

Daffodils cannot weep,
We presume, & so we think
Them merry—

Laugher of color & form—
Little knowing
What they feel,

Until shadow-flowers
Weep at the sun.

§

At the shadows of the edges of noon
Moons break
The page has an erection
It is a surface, having the form of a body
A terrain or interior
Gaze inflecting
What's not seen but merely
Heard of or imagined

If you imagine something, will it break?
If you sink into the weight of its reflecting
How will birds feel you?
& If you recover, what does it sound like
To be bleeding from the landscape
While noon wakes
& The page is the shadow of laughter?

§

The page is the opening
Into which we breathe
When our false selves are cinders

Ashes from breath
& Breath for our departing
In worlds that leave us blank

Blank like light
In the forbidden camera
In the anchor of the self, the selvage

Into which we are now stolen

§

It's too late for poems
We have distractions
Being nowhere but in between
While all of history trembles

Having bled into the camera
For art, if it were somewhere
Other than our complications
Which, seeing, then we leave

Toward what? A nonchalance
Preternaturally given
While the living world goes elsewhere
Outside the familiar

One lives inside where one is—
Blank land where we stir
Until dreaming the familiar
To awake but complicate

All history drawing blank

§

We don't mean anything. We never did.
We tire or grow distracted;
We aren't really here
When we're here. It's perplexing.

What would I have wanted
To say to them, if they had been here,
I mean really, not just present
But implicated in the surroundings?

Being here really palpably
In the marrow of living—
Is that something I have achieved
Or you, dear reader?

§

The wind with its decipherable eyes,
Its wicked intent, its bleakness.
Wind carries away the dust,
Binding your reflection.

In the wind you are here, though you don't
Mean it. The wind agrees
With your dislike of Michael Jackson, the song
Playing in the coffee shop, among

The lithographs crookedly hung.
The wind isn't here though. Wind entered
In a dream. In the dream you swore
You wouldn't tell me the

Dream. Only where we are is dreamlike,
Populated by imaginations,
Our blind imaginations, thick like birds
Who weep our bare reflections into dust.

§

Here, which is (still) not settled
Here, inside the dust where we aren't sure
Here, which is the ghost of an imagination, chaining
Here, until all silence meets its counterpart
Violent like here, which is not yet broken
Here, in the locations of dead birds
Here, which is already such sweet capture
Here, with eyes pertaining to tomorrow
Here, with flowers bleeding near your hand
Here, which has not ever been quite what we desire
Here, where we're asleep with quiet birds
Here, where you have chosen (not) to breathe
Unlike here, where we have really never been
Being now discharged ~~displaced~~ in front of
                    Everything & no one else ever again.

§

The stakes are greater when we breathe

Through phases of the wind,

Valley, in the sense of being still,

Places where we vary from the map.

The map places us inside its borders

It organizes space so we can't see

It locates us within a distance,

A palpable remains

It effaces all our tracks before

The edges of location

Knowing what's movable until it's too soon

Until the very Earth quakes & rambles, in the comfort of

                           [having been lost

§

The rain is a dull interloper;

It presumes to know your condition

For you; it wants to agitate

For any surprise; it wants

But it does not consume; it meditates
With passion, fully possessed of an idea—
With constriction, finally.
The wind is not so private

That you cannot hear her laughing
In your face as wet leaves pass,
Pissing your hair as trees stagger,
Drunk with such aplomb.

§

To rend the air in an open economy
Of birds & their squawking
As if the air meant to envelop you
Yes, really meant it, out of some unkindness

Define "the lyric." How can you?
I tried once, I suppose, but it was all just
Words on a page. Where an "image" is just a
Figuration

Deftly foregoing the "what" which
Tenderly we leave.

§

Location changes, effaces
Clouds & selves. In the root of
Moot, immovable objects bearing down.

Elsewhere is a disappearing claim,
A nonlocation with no name,
A placelessness with no desire,
The other of where we almost stood.

If we stand, poking
A toe in dry earth. If the
Bare sky gets caught in
Our hair, on jagged
Mountaintops—

Then move, through symbols
Of the drifted night
& In arid wind take flight
Toward dirt. Green land. Where we stand.

§

Locate the primitive
In your shoe,
Let it belong to you
As compactly as dust

Present yourself with a copy
Of belief
Let boredom gather where there is no grief
Let heat sing from the ledgers
Until the night rain is like music

If you believe, let clouds fall on you
Let midnight gather in your shoe
Let the rains belong to all of us
When you're stolen, in night air

§

The lyric is a *form* of thinking
As a map is a draft of place.
Farther than sand. We are
Farther than the night that sent you

To be released in a chorus of sighs
To move peripherally through the draft of a breakthrough
Is only to admit the existence of landscapes
Not to see through their perspective

To sing with grass in your teeth
To jostle in the mirth of gardens
Letting sun cling to your hair
Farther, farther from despair

§

One of the cacti, I think, is dead,
The one that sometimes bloomed late summer

It lies there like a bent submarine
I can hardly look at it

To bloom in riot of creation
Is to mock all easy dullness

Until distraction lingers
In the sadness at the edge of a page

§

In rainy afternoon light
A poem might be made of soggy trees
Of the pulp of leaves
Or dim cloudlight which lends the earth its mystery

In the valley of distraction
Listening to Robert Johnson
A poem might be made of anything
At which we now take place

———————————————

Clouds thicken, like a sentient
Distraction
Which lends false mystery
To the appearance of flowers & objects

Laugh, if you don't grope
Grope, if you're impervious to what yet should be
In dead heat of summer
With all the flowers laughing

Flowers which are layers
& Echo where they fill
If they don't grieve for imperfect amazement
While being dead all winter

Aren't we, still, too often
Dulled at noon's quiet flight
Until the self is angular
Hungry for alarm

§

Flowers which are layers
In your hair

§

"America's wandering away from me
in a dream of pine trees and clouds"
—Frank O'Hara

Sunlight on pine
Hymn chimes in windy
Opulence, sun strewn,
Blossoms' scent thick in air

⁓

A terrain is its own mind
It is a song pointed willfully
It is something you must "cover"— but how?
Carrying the dirt of earth on your soles

~

Nothing
But the day
Until it's night

~

What memories rattle
In the map you have made
Map you have put yourself into?

Does one wander in a map?
It is often difficult to refold, or find
A location such as 'G-4' in relation

To the ledge on which you are now standing
In afternoon's slight heat
With a broad map in the wind now rattling

~

All over
Is desire

A gossamer
Connector

Precondition
Of animal life

Over sea &
Land

Where we stand
Idle mammals

§

I don't know which way
To have begun
Is *song*, & the word leaves
Us rushing past light

Light is a condition
For the existence of crocuses
& Poppies & snapdragons
Daisies & thyme

All the world
Afloat in bloom
When you go out into noon
& The colors are a kind of savagery

We witness them, unable
To equal their intensity

Words are facts. Dusk. Butterfly.
Shadow. Umber. Edge. Encampment.
We feel their weight. We hold them
On the tongue

Never to be won.

§

In this place of trespass
Where we stood
As if meadow were a garment
A concordance of the senses
Jammed into location

At the ridge, where you clamber
To eke out a habitat
& We settle, naturally—
A place where we can touch & hear
The racket of birds' wings

In the rhythm of empathic glances
Tearing up the future
To root in dry earth
In this place where we are trespassers
& With all the windows shaking

§

In the nature of what's said,
A kind of garden
With you nearer the trespass
& Hilarity's accidents

As if I were supposed to
Feed you— sincerely.
But how? Here
Are these wildflowers,

Broken insect
Wings. Won't you
Make repast of them,
Then dig

Your fingers into cold

Wet soil— pull

The earth up by its

Hair?

Only if you dare.

§

Bullshit! I want the sun
& Accidents on display. I want
The fidgety shapes of bats
In flight— so common
At a summer's dusk—
Skittering about the skies
Smaller & more awkward than most
Birds. They don't make
Sounds that we can
Hear. Then they disappear
When we most fear them.

§

To be folded into twilight

Where all the lightning surged

Indiscriminate as a bolt or a flicker

Until we start describing

When we describe, we describe

What seems risible

Into unbalanced night

Where all the lightning sways

If you give, or you are given

Hunger is an introspection

& All the lightning pales

To the memory of that transcription

§

I seem to have lost track of standing

Here

In fragments of a position

With yellowjackets bobbing in the breeze

Yellow, bobbing grace

On your face

Think of swelter

Being one

& This place, a condition of
Color swollen—
Night as respite— & the crooked
Melodies of birds

Transition to a darker material—
Green & yellow-
Green
Leaves

Bobbing
In the wind—

§

To move in relation to skies which change suddenly
To rest in continent's drift & pull
To sing continually of the fate of the dissipated
To plant oak trees & sunflowers
To drive impatience to its core
To linger in the heat which will not bear us
To dive into the air or furniture (the future
        is uncoiled)
To clasp hands with a stranger
(Breath, implying breath will continue—

§

Blunt image
In the drift of now
Dark place
Jutting forward

A captive sampler
In the seen winds
Holds
A face to the terrace

The book an obsolete
Living
Material—
Staring at the given

If you
Are given
A book, place
Your hand on the receiver

If you receive
In terror sharper
Images of words
Don't look me in the ear

Look in your own, & fill it
With ungainly
Sights,
The city eaten up at night

The forest full of silence
The material at the edge of empty
Sight—
Tensile, almost full

§

At the edge of the material
Broken into laughter
Daring not to breathe
Or feel, with silence gashing

Into flames, with all
The inward material broken
Until we all fall down
In gash of what was flamed

§

The wind inflects
Its perception of cities
& Paltry human avenues
Deeper than we go

To go as placed
In the jutting atmosphere
Under clouded monuments
Larger than thought

It's funny, words wake
You up or put you
To sleep almost never
In between— an extreme

Of amazement hidden
Under the avenues
Where the wind does not go
Deeper than atmosphere

Larger than thought

§

The dance of branch &

Flower

Swaying in harsh winds—

Until all forms are lively, jutting

Accidents & speech—

To caress liltingly

As a song fracture

Until even evening blooms

In quick desire, hidden by alarm—

III

How to hide
In the presence of nuance
Still with winter's rumblings?

If we say what
We say, &
Rebegin   even then

        We're trapped in silence

Effigies
           Clinging to tomorrow

§

Being here, or given
To the mirth of not standing
In the way of whatever
Else is at hand

If we intend anything
It is to smirk
A little longer
'Til clouds get grayer

67

In the effortlessness of place inscribing
Dusk unto discovery
Dirt into the seed devising
Its own birth from whatever

Else is at hand

§

In the shunt of what is possible
Telling (as I thought on my morning run)
Not what's literally 'true,' but *true*
All the same. Never believe

Never believe in truth— or believe
Then find yourself hidden
Under discretionary neon
Which even flowers shun

§

"And he fails! He fails, that meditative man!"
—George Oppen

But does he, George? There are

Nothing but isolate men now, &

Women. You couldn't

Have foreseen it,

Breathing a fresh drop of Bay air &

Walking

Into history, which itself is

Full of desolation—

§

To be included

In the space of the dream

Which you are about to have

If you remember, or are asleep

If you consult with all dead forms

In the shapely verbs which inflict speech

While swaying in an ice storm

Vaguely remembering that the meaning of *digital* used to be

Having to do with the fingers

I have no fingers

The iPad has no keys

I've forgotten how to translate,

How to leave or isolate a dying species

In a place where dusk is almost full,

Where dreams erupt to gorge on human skin

      Like every place we've settled in.

§

> *"All those people up there in black suits taught*
> *not to let their feet tap. It's hopeless!"*
>   —*Clark Coolidge*

We could say, couldn't we, that living
        Is being in *motion*—

Even my cactus, Olson, sways
      (Gradually, over weeks)
Toward the course of the sun.

§

To be the father of no country
Awash in sinful parades
While thrushes fatten on spilled desire
& Hummingbirds grow shrill as chalk

On blackboards; then, to become emboldened
Soldiering among the crows
Who still dream of escaping the city
But fester amid playgrounds & landscaping

In the shadows of the callously thin.
To grow thin too, but be despoiled
At the moment of rebirth
At which all children are supposed to be lost

Like remaindered issues of magazines, or
Tattooed druggies who sneer as in cartoons;
Then to reappear, & almost mention fecundity
As long day drifts toward gentle evening—

§

The 'ancient dictionary' pulses
In a silence of dead
Tongues. If you want to
Weep,

You will find reason to
Weep. If you want to
Regard the heat &—
Heat in tremors, flinging

Death by syllabus or
Alibi,— clouds or
Chords, from the throats of hungry
Children— listen

To the peace which becomes rumor
Every time the hungry touch you, &
Your naked feet go dancing
Go in search of the one

Clear promise— reading &
Rereading— feeding
The evidence in vision of that flame.
To carry the heat

Again & again—

§

Then reading is a kind of ecology—
A bare mark of the need
                        To cultivate
This or that frail book—

                As if a tiny species
In a corner, in the shade—
        Fragile⁺ analog to human   hunger— in
                        This place where we aren't standing⁺⁺

   ⁺agile   ⁺fertile   ⁺rampant   ⁺profligate

   ⁺⁺surrendered, to what the dead can only carry

   ⁺⁺carried, like the dead to human need

                        —*after Jack Collom & Emily Dickinson*

§

Then to have come so far from this space of

Want I am behind myself—

That is the gift

The gift that forms the poem

Of goodbye.

Goodbye is a strain or behavior

Which cuts against the landscape.

Landscape wants all human animal &

Plant life to *cohere*

Against its strain, or very nature

Like a city waiting to be born

~~Unbuilt~~ in crevices of forest's shadow

Which is our nature, our marrow, our cutting

Geography— in the contingent lives of species like

Birdcries flinching

Until the abrasions of settlement are now deformed

By whispers rising here—

§

The world is contingent on whispered alibis,
Chalk hymns carrying the weight
Of no one
Left standing. If no one—

If no one is left standing;
If no one is a cloud or town, or
Something else visibly adrift. & If

You sketch it, writhing
In waves being no one,
Nowhere ever to be lost

Or here— or being no one left standing
While bearing the weight of whispered clouds.—
& If someone—

The statutory emblem of goodbye—
Looked at you— gnawed
At your shadow— entered
Your veins until delight

Leaked down
Your fingers.—

Who is the first charge?
Who the last? & Who is stolen
From this measure, this

Alibi, this slinking departure
Clasped in the weight of its shadow? Who—
Who the interlocutor? Who the receiver

Of these strange transmissions, on which
All earthly life depends?—

§

Then to go down still, in this birth of finding
You here, like a flower,
A flicker, lilting dearth of modern
Tongues—

Tongues which devour
Us— devour, & yet capture
All our fears;
To drill, in fear of flowering;

To drill, unto the hearts of azure cities;
To drill until even the road leaks
Oily reek across the barren plain.—
If you come here, do not seek

Deliverance from birth;
Bend down instead, kiss
The dust when no one's looking— kiss
The fragile earth goodbye.—

§

Loveliest can be caught in a burnt-out maw
In the shape of wild desire
In the shape of wild— is loveliest—
Loveliest itself a burnt-out now, a stolen
      Petal of corrosive
      Touch [*touch* rhymes with *torch*]

To sear the air like **victory** ~~flesh-smell~~
To saturate the earth like secret chemicals
      in earth's muscles,
Like the nouns we cannot use to name all ruin
Leaching now beneath our random feet.

If you have feet— use them;
Get down to the core;
Make others run— make lists;
Memorize, & burn, then study them.

What the poem is is a concordance of such lists,
A quiet replica,
A master plan thick with the dust of former selves
~~'Til the air starts burning—~~

    & We embrace these lists like old lovers, firestorms—
    Like places where we run but don't cohere
    'Til, spurned like dusk on the flight of wires & selves,
        We grow clarified by others in our wake.—

§

The poem is running late for its own recital
It could stagger, but just doesn't care
To write a rich man's epitaph
While hired into doom

To be frightened into speech is not to chatter
But to sing like a drowned man awakening
Driven, after tides, from ruined chords
Until even our own shadows are not breathing

§

I don't know anymore
The here which is
Placid & familiar
As anything else which has already been stripped bare

An image of sex in the trees
To sing what is real upon rooftops
Which are still not accessible by normal degrees
Even here, where we are quaintly familiar

& Sing, upon hilltops
When we are otherwise flitting
& Everything else has already been said
In the very air that clings to us like smoke

§

Sky is the reverse
Map of trees &
Buildings
Whose faces are cut out—

A reverse cartography of neon
Grafting noon to
Clockfaces— reflections' swoon
To silver ponds.

The night-sky blusters
At the crooked
Mountains sweeping effortless
Effortless peace through the trees.

§

Writing with improper ink
What do my hands desire?
A fate worse than rain?
The means of forging a proper blowout?

Fate is offkey

At the root of all sunday schools

Until desire is a fragile run-on

& The dictionary laughs at dust

Retailing an improper blowout

In earth's imperfect, tactile mystery

§

SELF: Earth's no mystery. Everything you can say of it could be written on a fig. Bland or fabricated, *like how's your evening going?*— a question which deserves nor courts a serious response.

SOUL: That earth came to be, & continues, being, somehow, despite our, yes, collective rapacity, mysterious & gleaming, as the full moon the other night. Do we expect grandeur, on a scale beyond capacity & height? Who can imagine an ocean? Are there words which fly like bullets from the sun?

SELF: The earth is raw, rough, unpolished, seen & unforeseen, bold, slippery, sharp & wet, cold & blazing, all at once. The earth is fickle as a lover, & as arid as these words we'd use to describe her (Earth). Such words are never fleeting, never quick. They stay too long, like those who think they can describe a world (such vast continuum!) in terse, sure sentences, clogging our perceptions, making us forget what it's like to breathe or be *awakened by an idea.*

SOUL: But earth's very hardness, I think, is part of what you complain about— not the fact, but the idea— & it doesn't exclude flickering mystery, any more than perception precludes thought, or love desire.

SELF: Who are you, a ghost in whom I don't believe, to lecture me on fact, or love, or truth?

SOUL: Not to lecture, I hope, but telling the truth.

SELF: But truth, you know, is such slippery stuff.

SOUL: & This is just what makes it food for poetry. You could, as easily, slip on a rock in December.

SELF: If one would climb at all.

SOUL: We all climb the ideas of our choosing, or else sulk on an unworthy perch.

SELF: Who are you ghost, who bests me at the sins of my delight?

SOUL: You might call me the *duende*, as Lorca did.

SELF: Or muse, or Other, if such distinctions matter?

SOUL: They don't, even if they are false, as death is long.

SELF: But who then, Monster!—

SOUL: Think of me as the Sun in Mayakovsky's poem—

SELF: & So O'Hara's?

SOUL: Yes, but with a dash of what Lorca perceived.

SELF: Then you will haunt me?

SOUL: Haunt, or visit you—
   So that matter can more plainly come to view.

§

Is space a condition of having been seen,
Just like life's a condition of being in it

All the time? Here, the bruiting
Sun blares down your ear. How much air

Does it take to form a clearing? How much
Breath to form a poem? How many stars

To offset the lights of cities
Burning, like there was never night, nor air?

§

The cities always burn. Men stand in them
Lamenting suddenness. When you get to the end
Of the page, you have two choices. Cities
Burn up everything we need. Don't listen
To me; I live in a city

Of sorts. Just stand there fingering

Your desire for hunger & worthlessness

Like a child who has gone suddenly

Astray, to darker climes, where bees aren't still.

Whenever you're told you have just two choices,

Don't believe it. The end of the page burns away,

Creating a new edge, impertinent as the future.

The page, like the city, is a myth we have made

Where cities burn what we don't need;

Then gather up what's stolen

Until your fingers bleed.

§

> "Even if there's a gigantic flash flood. Even if my codex is swept
> [away,
> it is all my brain. And I'll have it. Even if the world is gone."
> —Alice Notley

I enter language in order to change it, & be changed.

That's a lie: I haven't changed anything. (Am I changed?)

All the dumb medals in all the dead tongues

Weigh too much for my feet to engage.

Poetry isn't necessarily 'true'— but *is* the truth.

Poetry isn't necessary?

Poetry's necessary, in its wild surprise,

Its trumpeting abandon.

Do the dead need poetry? Do ghosts care

More than their shadows in the awakening air?

This planet's not a shadow. Earth's

A fragile macrostructure, blue

Habitation in the densest air

Imaginable— a lucky yarn or prism

Of desire— or wealth which has been squandered,

Squandered by fool heirs,

Just like in Shakespeare. The glares of the bees encapsulate

A history of speech-

lessness— one (it sometimes seems) has

A language in order masturbate. Whereas

Reading is a deep blue cloud. Having

Become a language,

A language & a conflagration, in the conflicting

Trees. The language I speak of (if I seek

Anything) isn't always blue.

Unless it's startled by useless thunder, a need for wanton

Closure. Could I be truly wanton,

If I fell apart

Outside the heroes of interesting tongues?

Today was violent, but not yet anything

Repressed like speech. We have been here before

All the time, like our blue selves, always

Triggered, restlessly contained, with everything

Always new at stake. I have

Nothing new or beautiful

To tell you. In this

Still-constructed story

Of our futures, leave

Out all our deaths, & how I side

With you, brave amigo,

True witness to our still-ironic days,

& Bearer of all false-true promises,

Or else just damned good company

In this new, diminished century

At which even brave poets are not heeded.

for Anselm Hollo

§

If you study exhaustion, it will laugh at you,

Clog your sentences with unneeded

Syllables,

& Grimace at your stammer. If you invite

Exhaustion to your gala dinner,

It will yank devices from the belts

Of the confused. If you incite

Exhaustion, it will descend on you,

Making you lisp & quiver. You can't quote

Exhaustion, for its speech is intolerable,

Even to itself. Exhaustion hovers

At the perimeters of meetings, reciting

Memos to the weary.

Exhaustion can't live here

Or anywhere but on your back

& Neck, driving its weight into

Your muscles' depth,

& Overhanging your brow

Magisterially, as if one of Baudelaire's

Own "crushing chimeras"

Of whose burden, the bearers— dim

Men lurching— seem

Preternaturally unaware.

§

The horizon disappears into the slant

Of an idea. Sunlight decomposes in the evening

When young men laugh. The future is occupied

In a fissure or atmosphere

Where the wicked die of leaving. If

You live, please do not be deceived.

'Nature' is an idea, a word coined in half-hearted

Attempt to describe the phenomenal

World. The phenomenal world cannot be described;

'Nature poetry,' thus, does not exist; & if you write

A 'nature poem,' you create a bare

Shadow of the landscape— a barren, handmade thing.

The landscape is more various

& Fragile than your vocabulary, whoever you are, & whatever

Words you know. Words

Are like trumpets or triggers, things

Made by men, or women. Words

Are determined by your future, your incomplete

Or past selves— but nature's

A huge bundle

Of variousness on the verge of slipping
Off a cliff. Doesn't this
Bother you? Is there
Blood in your veins? Do you feel
Sexual, at least sometimes? Doesn't anything
Excite you, or are you just taking up space— space
Of which there's far too little?

for Jack Collom

§

Because you are going, & then coming back
I can still flick the slumber from my bones
While heat runs away
In unremitting day
At which you & I still reside

Because you are not breathing in a state of departure
Where neon laughs at you, & flesh grows
Static; because the light seems pale
As your assorted, fleshly selves,
Am I dreaming in a grotto where we meet.

What does one say in a grotto?

Festooning is hilarious, if done wickedly
Your eyes wring out the fire from the sun
& Are led through winter's pale contractions
At some wicked curvature of delay
Until Autumn laughs at you.

Don't breathe— just watch the jittery
Flight of bats at dusk. With noon's
Still eyes escaping amber light;
Then flee, unto the night while moon escapes
Dawn's violent birdcries.

IV

The environment itself is almost full
It haunts like all dead structures
It clarifies our speech while still not slipping
Its wickedness is like a summer orgy

Which we aren't party to
Though it hastens the pull of dead summer moons
Through crumpled heat
In shrill digressions where things aren't scarified

If you can heft a dynamo, breathe
Through the comportment of the skin
Through windows at the back of your tongue
If you can do anything else, awaken

Stare violently into night
Fall out of windows while love takes flight

§

To be a part of everything that color can express—

Rich orange of the poppies, or

Purplish wildflowers I don't know—

But to be embedded, in such craggy

Vividness

Even at evening when the light disperses

& All colors are places

Of shadow & delight

Which the moon does not suspect—

& If mountains forged your

Vocables,

How would color slide down your throat

In cool air, without stars, under

The shadows of the bees?

———

The heat's a boring plume which stays all day but has to go away. (If you're reading this in winter, imagine an unbearable sauna experience.) Color lies at the edges of experience. Does my cat really see the same pale carpet's blue as I do? Or that electric fuchsia of flowers, in my neighbor's balcony garden? The moon doesn't suspect much, but the mountains will outlive us. Stick out your tongue & catch song. Become undone by tender rattlings of the stars.

§

Like small birds scarified at dusk
By whom we are tormented
I am witness to all shadows flitting
In the company of neon

The birds themselves do not care
For shadow—
Only the drowsy air seems pertinent
To their capillaried vision

In the air, where you can sometimes swarm
If you aren't careful
With such contingent & divergent scratchings
As only flowers bear

§

In the heat, which drinks up all your breath
Which decimates horizons
& Drenches your dry tongue
While shadows flee this complicating mirth—

Heat is vested in the scorch of the primitive—
In body, which is source
Of its own fire, even at light's ascendancy
In pale hours we are held by reckless birth—

Go in heat then, to be hidden
In a primitive tree— a collage of stifled
Dust. In this place, dripping with wildness
Here you will sacrifice your tongue in order to

See, or surrender, like the scars
Rippling across your muscles
Which sear you, scare you, leave you burned
& Burn the very poem into flesh— astride

The hungry, daylit world

§

It is necessary to continuously disrupt oneself
It is impossible, in the swelter of neon
It is important to smirk, but not appear   to be doing so
Or flower, in the weight of summer's clutching

It is impossible continuously to reinvent
Oneself
But important to appear to be furnishing
The place with all disrupted material—

Put your hands up to mirror's contested
Territory
Track your voice years from now
& Mend, like impermanent summers

Flowering miles
Impacted by days' pale limits
Broken telepathy
If you want to become more than the weight of your shadow

Swilled by dusk toward violent becoming
'Til all flowers are wickedly forged
In freshets of the interior
While evening slips & burns—

§

Here, or teeming
In the construction of birdvoices
Which burn the billowing
Atmosphere.

Listen
To the silence which burns
Their throats. Listen
To the silence which

Rises
From your center.
Listen to the center of your dream—
If you dream, as either

Rioter or witness,
Reinvent yourself in summer's swift
Discharge.
Dream in riots of color laughing—

Until all heat has been ejaculated
From the edges of your tongue.

§

Everywhere, having to go, betokened
In the company of on-
lookers I am not beholden
To—

The ecological lightbulb
Flickers, thinking
Itself in some hor-
ror flick

The world isn't about to go
Away
Necessarily— yet
The world isn't
'About'—

Hold your tongue;
It slips out, doesn't
It?— & yet the trees
Awakened when in flower

Are still parts of a
Dis-
cursive e-
conomy of shadows

Where the still parts are
To curse
This witness— straining
At the seine

Culture as nature, an outright
Stick— or echo
Chamber
Where the future leaves
Off—

"*Your* future," as once was
Sung, &
"No future," the way we
Keep going—

§

What about the time is night wasted

Night I cannot use or exchange

If I want to confirm it

Like dead walks old men make

Night I can't undo while it's still clenching

Night which caresses your ankles like I would

I am tired of the night & its surface cohesion

Its surface of the poem where the angels won't conform

There are no angels, so they won't confirm

Anything at a distance hidden

Between earth & its names

Between naming & the horizon at the apex of the page

The page is not an animal landscape

But mimics its uncertainty

Its hairtrigger shrillness, its echo

Of plant & animal names

In the afterlife of what's been spent

Or spilled here, at the entrance

To the night ~~night, which cannot be entered~~

~~But enters us like silent cargo~~

Like forms of mimicking in the distance
Like traces of entrancement— dead birds leaving
Semen in the trees
Or anything else unpronounceable

At the limits of your feet where shadows ache
Where the seeds of night are spoken
& We become incapable of stuttering
In the afterlives of poems— or anything else we leave behind

§

How could we be there when they could disarm us
In their wrath which is the color of very dark pearls
Against the sky, in the night we would abandon
If it weren't so obvious?

The treason of the window disengages.
I want to sing a light tune, nothing fancy,
Nothing shrill.
   The body edges

From the dream which had been afflicting
It— to linger at the outskirts of an event,
Seized by wild reason
Which the vividness of daylight overturns.

§

The landscape is not the page
But we thrive on its capacity
To change shapes as thriftily as a bee resolves
To ransack your renewed sense that what is being done

Is far too little, if anything
Could undo this need to cling to an horizon
But still not venture upward
In the unsettling surround

If you are surrounded, forget who you are
If you're here, then get behind me
Run away for awhile, yet stay excited
While light carefully unfolds in evening's plumes

§

The hive collapses
Cities collapse
We've learned to dive, or cover
Ourselves in permeable ink—
The ink in which
Our poems are now written

The hive collapses
While collapsible selves
Disarm us with their banter
If you're going to go ~~asleep~~ go now
Even when we are not here
Awake in scenes which forcibly
Are emoted—

The hive collapses
The birds now all are outside, singing
Every manner of beak's jabber
A trill or an outburst
In the boring, defined confines
Of a city which only bursts
Out rarely
But seldom actually collapses
Unlike Lana Turner

Whom I'm not really interested in as an actress
Although she did live in a 'hive'
Of sorts, as do most of us mammals
Before we truly collapse
Nurtured by disaster
Until pesticides leach from our own backsides
Ever after
Ever after

§

Yellow leaves
Swirling bright
In afternoon light

Is the memory
Of an hour lost
Greater than the extraction

Of heat by complicit
Desire
Desire yellow, swirling bright

Too swiftly

In afternoon

Light?

§

Nothing of living imagines that we write

The arid earth cannot conceive a page

Desire usurps word for object

Hunger, a raw itch which often leads us to devour

Can life itself not equal poetry?

We who shunt from paycheck to dislocation

Find rare hours in bloom

Where helpless people are not lowing

Nothing of breath necessitates delight

Air unlike desire's democratic

It will not resist what you most need

Yet it leaves you futile, unfulfilled

Nothing of writing implicates desire
Yet poetry is lust itself
Written in forms not yet imagined—
Or reimagined— which we keep remembering

Until breath itself must go

§

What becomes sayable
Resonates in the bones
Of the ear, saying *what*
Or swaying

To say or to sing
Are the same anything—
We experience them at edges
Of unimagined buildings

The buildings we imagine
Populate laughter
With doppelgängers & interstices
Too greedy to bleed

To sing, expanding what you say
In an ear or a twig
Full of stale everythings—
Everything you've now forgotten that you know

§

Here, as in waking
In breath or cleft air
Hearing mutable   bird voices
In states of laughter

The self knows more than you fear
It does   writing in states of
To grasp— lacking relevance
Or compose thought balloons

To indifferent species
Entering thought   inhabiting
It, the false   relevance
Of mask & emergency

The self knows more than you fear it—

Or moves, if you don't

Determine its position

Sufficiently, in gardens

When the mind is everywhere

Amused / confused / speciated

Toward laughing emergencies

Until the self is a thought balloon

Which you fear, while not hearing it

§

Poetry must implicate pleasure, at least tangentially. The pleasure that I fear goes deep below my eyes. As we dissolve in white spaces where noise is shattered. & Your eyes, so full of where the dark grief of eyes grows full. Your eyes, a blight of winter's thinness. A biosphere of trumpets & loose change. To rhyme in flight of onlookers who'll soon scatter, blinking in just such a way as to seem casual, almost fierce. The fierce incisions which are my eyes take me where the poem needs to go. Within scenes of mirrors entering facts, while habitation clings to our bulky appointments. & We grasp at skies like some more worldly Icarus, twisting in the neon breeze.

§

If I plunge
Or know you, almost

           The digital
           Effaces
      Signs
Previously scrawled into papyrus

     Eroding record
          Needing
          No disk space

Just endless witness   of desire
    Carved into night air

V

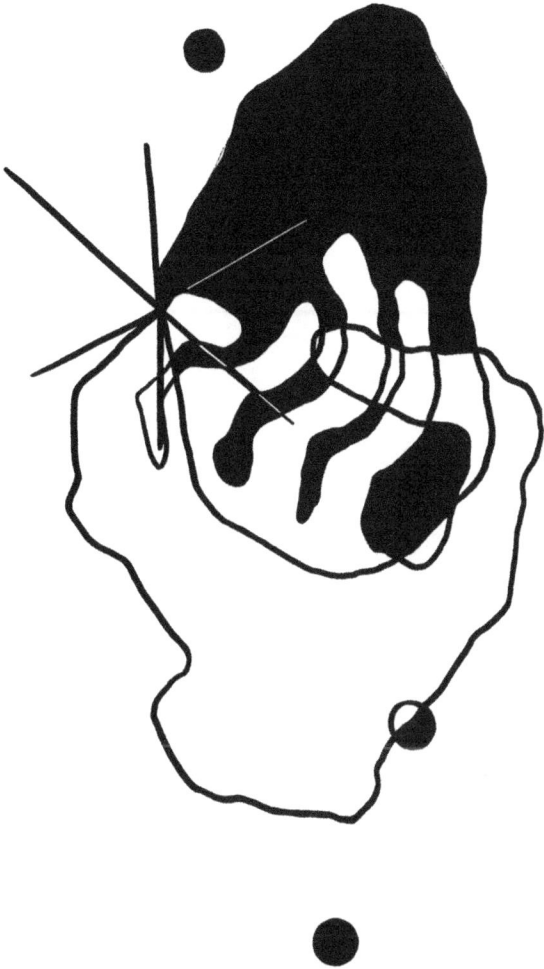

How to map it, the book, the
Topography of what's left out, the
Strangeness of words on a page, if you
Can touch them, if you could turn

In fright? The world is rampant interchange,
An intersection of the known & darkly
Broken. Cold artifact, in a place
Where memory is lapsed shadow

& In flits of rampant screenlight
Somehow less than speech or air.

§

> *"in the great mouth that has lost speech"*
> —*César Vallejo (trans. Clayton Eshleman)*

In the sunlight, which divides us
In the echo of what doesn't translate
In the silence where we aren't reflected
But can be seen, persistently, needlessly
Humming without thought

In this unseasonable mild December

In a clinch, where we are not mistaken

For someone's lover, in a dream state

In which one often falls

From a great height, into doom

In the nearness of what fills

Us with delight

In the long run, it will be forgotten

In the wind, where we don't listen

To the children chanting singsong rhymes

Into the empty street, toward which

Even strangers do not pass

§

The page refuses

To be occupied

It is a spatial

Form of amazement

Thus far, in the breach

A confinement which intensifies
When speech is almost full

~

When the page is empty or agitating
For its self-determination, its profligacy

The page is a terrain, a complex
Ecosystem of exchanges

To keep pace with erasure
Amid location's rupture

Lie down in the space of page-like
Constraints

Echoing the echo

~

To be lost now, in the echo
& In cities which enable it

Dank spaces which   ruin the infinite
Corruption of speech always already   underway

As if one dreamed along the ocean floor
& All its possible reflections

The ancient horses are laughing
At the smell of windows broken

Dusk, a violent thunderstorm of color
Whose possibilities weep

Of index cards or phone bills or intractable summer outings

~

Biting the interior's
Sharp canopies, we enter
Bruised. transformed. transformative

On the brink, impervious to neon clues
Which once we'd settled for

To be lost now, in the echo

& In cities which enable it

When even poetry is not enough

~

Thinking, in remembered cities

While being the president of a state I can't construct

But from which I'm, preternaturally, about to set sail

If I become a character

In my own awakening; if I am to become part of

A world I must set right

Or create; if I am about to fill anything

With its own disregard; if I want

What I want, but can't become

Listless with perturbation; if I care

Being almost caught

At an investigative body

Which you scatter

Until noon rubs off.

§

In habitations where we breed
& Gather in order to slip into
Night, or its song fractures
Further than desire

If desire is a station
With the wind & bare trees spilled
Out from just under a tremor
Where we bloom & swerve

Back, though intermittently
Stilled by revenant strictures
Which flicker & lurch in frozen doom—
In the earth & light disappearing

§

Dear Sender, don't go in

The window is occupied

The limits of its breath reveal

A state of transitive

Arousal.

When the state is occupied, as it almost always

Is

Remember, as it remembers

Being swollen with mirth

Lacking dreams of stateless birth

If only for an hour

Until we accept what the skies are

Primitive & useless in flight

When everything else is already being revealed

§

At the edge of a departure

        Silence leaks

From our fingertips—

     & The trees

Barren specters

       Wisps in the sky

Laugh at us, eking

          Ground-bound

Hagglers aggrandizing

     Inhuman lust

       The whip of the future, what's

Still

  slip-

    ping

§

In this place where we do not return

To the condition of being in

If that is the case   if

We are 'placed' here

& 'Place' is a means, a position
Under the atmosphere
Returning formerly to the conditions
On which all fragile life's sustained

If we   if we return, or are in place
Not to 'stand in   place,' but a means
Of activity, placing   oneself
At the edge or point of returning

To a condition, former or future
Cumulous but not accumulating
Viabilities of stun
Fracture in a meadow or lane

A tangible slip, almost missing

§

To gather up what's not sustained, except in dreams;
To empty out the weather of its clangor;
To circle round the essence; to have used
Up one's ideas in
        the first book
& Still write twenty more; to glean an extent
Toward which what we
       mean's determined
By words or constructions
Available to us; to consider history as
A substance or essence
Accreting within; to consider history
As substance
       abiding in the landscape, shaping
Its capacities ~~history~~
        ~~as pollutant?~~;
To know how to mean anymore,
Absent constructions or
        soundbytes;
To be haunted by the landscape,
Its strictures & essences;
To swirl, determined by environs,
Surrounded by 'cool' people
Who only talk about money;
To scatter at the very limits of
The 'book,' its
       outskirts & wild
    surprises;
Then to end in song, before it's
        even begun;—

§

It begins, without even being
Near anything. It begins the randomness
We don't question, but should.
It begins in unvettably blue terrain,
In a clearing haunted by machinery.
It begins when we have emptied
Our minds of expectations
Of whether it will even begin, or how.
It begins & ends when poetry
Does— at instants where you want to
Savor a sentence, or grasp its palpable
Impulse.
        It begins when it begins,
& Does so again, constantly
Changing. It is too much for you to *ask*
To know when it begins. When it begins,
Being a part of the landscape where it is
Beginning, always anew. Some die for
Harbingers, trinkets of old money,
But beginning's not so much being born
As being thrown into a scenario.
        To begin: jumping in wind's teeth.
Beginning's logical: it necessarily precedes the end.

§

i.

So now you'll be returned

                To earth

To the still-bright mystery of what's   outside us

To the everything our bodies drift

           Between

Traces   lying just beyond

                Our grasp

ii.

Running this morning   brilliant

      Cold air   heavy heart

You are returning

         To the source;

You are

        Returning—

     Let trees sprout

From your flesh, your   ashes—

        Let the trees—

Let trees sprout, which grow poems

         In all languages

All the languages of this dying earth

Whose paths you've traced   ~~graced~~—

iii.

The time for poetry
          Is ~~almost~~ now—

The cat threw up
     Near the pile
Of Anselm books, not
On it—

          Paying her respects

          ~

The time for poetry
Is the times we live in

          ~

The time for poetry   is hard to find

For we

   Stray mortals, clutching   senseless

               Senseless, at the moon

        iv.

& We here, foolish beings

       Who agitate against   delight

In the fertile mystery of all that night   implies

          When we are "guests of space"

& There is nothing left   to do

But mourn   or write

   Into the night, where we

          Are shaken

        v.

The email's subject   tells me to "act now"

        But it doesn't tell me how

Now you

Are gone, dear friend

O wicked end   those fuckers

Bush, Cheney, & all the   others

Still alive, while you

        With more heart & dignity in your shoe—

Those well-polished shoes   —o wicked end

       vi.

Yet still what wickedness   that you   aren't here—

   Again, like a bear in the

      "Word forest"

Who eats   eats hungry leaves   slipping

       Stolen, in night air—

          Anselm Hollo: 1934 – 2013

§

      "No, we can't win. Give my love to the sunrise."
          —Rita Hayworth in Lady from Shanghai

Having lost my way,

I have nowhere to run but upward

Toward what sunrise,
What abrasive economies
Where the air doesn't sing?

When you sing, you should rush
Toward the site where the evening
Sun dissipates

In the colors of frozen trees— in the
Noncolors
Of new snow— in

The dirt we will be buried

§

An error occurred. A prompt monitor
Filled up with lightning.
        The interior is a mirror
Unto which we speak.

§

The lives of those we often miss
When touching
Like an aborted camera—
A flicker
A shadow on a page or face
Becoming ghost in the process of emptiness
Becoming

§

Those for whom the mind revolves
Like silence formed of breathing—

Those under the letters
Who sing in the bones of your face,
Who rampantly, rampantly are not here

Yet move
Through air, brokenly

To catch like breath in your hair

§

I become writing again   waging
Windswept grace
          Of place

It's all over my shoe
                  & You—

        The brain
        On the Internet
        Is a tiny
        Bubble

What does yours do?

         Integral windmills

The rapture of falling skyward

Williams was right, you know,
  About Imagination

        The plutocracy of the future
    Is here, insect-sinister

Will the "festival" be festive?

      Is there room in the town that you
  Storm out of?

In tiny intricacies of laughter

        Paroxysmal downsides

  Pale dusk-blue a kind of

Stop-motion gaiety

I shouldn't be writing

I pause long enough to clinch
        A whisper

     I shouldn't
         I shouldn't be writing

§

Being here, one isn't serious
It is a complex balance
Between frivolity & tenderness, the need
To affix the present

Within a steady narrative
Into which we've disappeared.
When the narrative disappears, improvise
When the

Cities are erased, make friends
With distance. When the nude
Horizon's swallowed by your palm
Cup your hands, blow into them

Until you're able to keep warm

§

Sunlight catches a gleam a horrific
Minute lost in comfort
We are attuned to but don't register
Beyond the animal level toward
Which we surrender
When we do, or double back
Upon transient surface housing
Then shiver or get lost
Subtracting what we need the most

§

To be here in irregular
Desire motions us
     To part / be part of
To burst through, in analogy-ecology
Until not needed
     By the past

The past is a myth
We reinstate
     By our intractable pursuits.
  The past needs us, unsteady
Recruits toward the sayable

Outside the visible, you're dead as salt

You, who do not move me

     Into complementary fractures

On which all rhythm & light depend

§

Grace, to continually
Burn in a moment—
A contingency we're tethered
To, as minutes written on rain
Going back to the
Start, to the
Part we call
Desire—

~

Desire is the first
Form, the start, the instigation
Moving in windows of tune
To annihilate rain

When we take
Breath in, when we
Remember our fingers
Or leave them in the air

When we drown, or seem imprisoned
Impregnated by our eyes
At an instant of erogenous
Breathing— when everything else falls away

When everything else falls, in the
Eradication of what we seek
When we seek delight,
In breath, where everything else holds sway

& We fall out of tune—

§

Sometimes, under the empty trees
Where birds escape

Where heat gathers, & is
Dispersed

Sometimes, will I lie
Dreaming of my past, my future

In the quiet 'here' of a summer's breach
Toward which dreams have been fastened

coda

How did I plan to end it?
& What have I even learned
In the false mystery which builds by comparison
As night fills with speculative nearness. So it is

Not resolved? It is not
Resolved. Yet what do I need still
From this poem, allegedly about
The OUTSIDE, which is inside too, & also

Dear as wonder that all fools reject
As we refuse to float unto infinity
But stay resolutely HERE
In this place, where skies are burning.

Boulder, Colorado
2011-2013
revised subsequently

Acknowledgments

Parts of this work have appeared, at times in slightly different versions, in the following journals:

Altered Scale: "Fact or rust," "To evaporate like speech, exchanging," "The terrain is an obvious patch," "The landscape, in fact, does not rush away," "It's better to write something brief, imperfect."

Big Bridge: "Sunlight on pine," "In this place of trespass," "Here, or clods of them," "If you study exhaustion, it will laugh at you," "Being here, or given."

Bombay Gin: "I enter language in order to change it, & be changed," "So now you'll be returned."

Eccolinguistics: "We don't mean anything. We never did."

New American Writing: "The environment itself is almost full."

On Barcelona: "The book is upside down!" "If I were a river I would flow," "To get through to the back," "When the moon falls on my heat or trousers."

OR: "To go on making faces at the screen," "Yet being here is exactly the," "It's too late for poems," "To breathe while singing other devices," "The stakes are greater when we breathe," "Location changes, effaces," "To be given wholly," "Locate the primitive," "The lyric is a form of thinking," "I seem to have lost track of standing," "To be a part of everything that color can express," "The cities always burn," "The horizon disappears into the slant."

About the Author

Mark DuCharme is the author of more than twenty books and chapbooks, including five previous full-lengths: *The Unfinished: Books I-VI, Answer, The Sensory Cabinet, Infinity Subsections*, and *Cosmopolitan Tremble.* Other recent publications include *Scorpion Letters*, forthcoming from Ethel, and his work of poet's theater, *We, the Monstrous: Script for an Unrealizable Film*, published by The Operating System. His poetry has appeared widely in such venues as *BlazeVOX, Blazing Stadium, Caliban Online, Colorado Review, Eratio, First Intensity, Indefinite Space, New American Writing, Noon, Otoliths, Shiny, Talisman, Unlikely Stories, Word/ for Word*, and *Poetics for the More-Than-Human World: An Anthology of Poetry and Commentary.* A recipient of the Neodata Endowment in Literature and the Gertrude Stein Award in Innovative American Poetry, he lives in Boulder, Colorado.

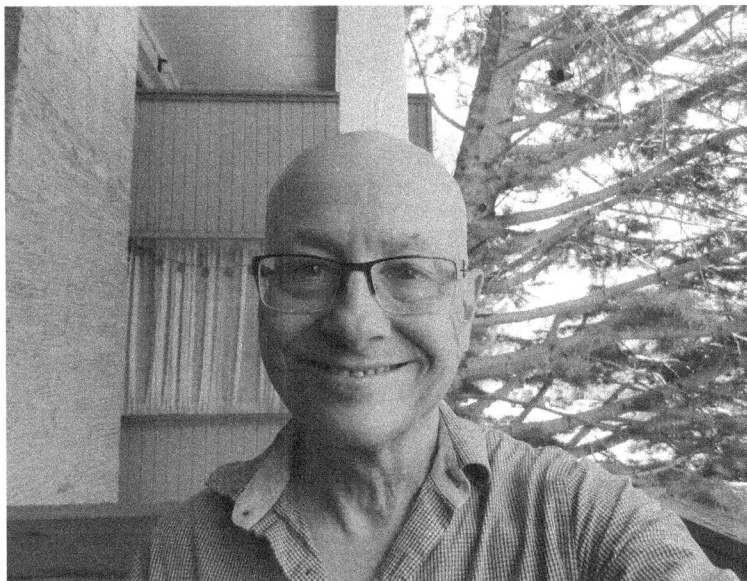

Other Books by Mark DuCharme

Life Could Be A Dream (last generation press, 1990).

Emphasis (:that:, 1993).

i, a series (Burning Press, 1995).

4 sections from Infringement (Oasis Press, 1996).

Contracting Scale (Standing Stones Press, 1996).

Infringement (Light and Dust, 1998).

Three Works (Invasive Map) (Oasis Press, 1998).

Desire Series (Dead Metaphor Press, 1999).

Near To (Poetry New York/Meeting Eyes Bindery, 1999).

Anon [with Anselm Hollo, Laura E. Wright and Patrick Pritchett, with illustrations by Jane Dalrymple-Hollo] (Potato Clock Editions, 2001).

Cosmopolitan Tremble (Pavement Saw Press, 2002).

The Sensory Cabinet | A Bit of Hades [with Anselm Hollo] (Left Hand Series 1, 2004).

Infinity Subsections (Meeting Eyes Bindery, 2004).

Inappropriate Content | The War of The End of The World [with Elizabeth Robinson] (Left Hand Series 14, 2006).

The Crowd Poems (Potato Clock Editions, 2007).

The Sensory Cabinet (BlazeVOX Books, 2007).

The Found Titles Project (Ahadada, 2009).

Answer (BlazeVOX Books, 2011).

The Unfinished: Books I-VI (BlazeVOX Books, 2013).

Counter Fluencies 1-20 (The Lune, 2017).

We, the Monstrous: Script for an Unrealizable Film (The Operating System, 2018).

Scorpion Letters (Ethel, 2022).

Recent Titles from Unlikely Books

www.ingramcontent.com/pod-product-compliance
Lightning Source LLC
Chambersburg PA
CBHW031853090426
42741CB00005B/467